The fascinating cloister of the Collegiate Church.

that have been eroded and tarnished by the passage of time. The sky had clouded over and small drops of rain were falling; a rural odour rose up from below and the town seemed to exude a distinct melancholy. The bell of the Collegiate Church, which was ringing at the time, augmented the effect of the pilgrim's surroundings.... All these things reached back to the past: Campo de Revolgo, with its tranquil sounds of trees and fountains; the silent monasteries that guard the town's entrance, predisposing the traveller with their grave calm; the venerable Collegiate Church towering over the crowded, tumbledown hamlet; the dilapidated towers and decrepit façades; the austere countryside, the silent township...."

In the 19th century, Víctor Fernández de Llera, a poet of the province of Santander *(montañés)*, expressed the town's melancholy charm in octosyllables:

> *¡Ay! ¡Qué sola entre las gentes!*
> *¡Qué sola estás, Santillana!*
> *¿Qué se hicieron tus abades?*
> *¿Qué tus gentes ermitañas?*
> *¿Qué fue del Marqués insigne*
> *por las musas y las armas?*

("Oh, how solitary among peoples! / How alone you are, Santillana! / What became of your abbots? / What of your

The Collegiate Church: main front.

A TOWN OF HIDALGOS

Santillana del Mar lies in a valley surrounded by hills, about 7 km north-west of Torrelavega and 30 km by road from Santander. Of all the towns and villages in Spain, it is perhaps the one whose ancient personality has best been conserved in the present-day appearance. The ensemble of the buildings and surrounding area has been declared a National Monument.

Previously the capital of Asturias, Santillana del Mar was the cradle of a large proportion of the noblemen of Castile. Many emblazoned houses survive, with escutcheons and heraldic devices relating to the most illustrious Castilian lineages, such as the Velarde Ceballos, Salazar, Barreda, Tagle, Calderón de la Barca, Peredo or Estrada families.

The name Santillana comes from the town's patron saint, Santa Illana. Legend has it that the Saint's remains were moved there in the 6th century, and that for this reason the place began to be called "Asturias de Santillana."

Santillana del Mar is a "museum of architecture," no less. One cannot take a step in the evocative, clean, lovingly cared-for streets without admiring the sight of a beautiful façade with a time-honoured coat of arms carved in stone, or of a poetic corner of the town with the green countryside appearing behind.

1

Pantocrator dating from the late 12th century.

Apart from the numerous monuments (indeed, the whole town constitutes a beautiful, varied monumental complex) and the landscape that frames the town, Santillana is furthermore of interest by virtue of its fascinating history. All these factors have aroused the literary interest of many writers, both Spanish and foreign, from Alain-René Lesage, the author of the novel *Gil Blas de Santillane* (first published in 1715, and translated from French to Castilian by Padre Isla), even to Jean-Paul Sartre, who has one of the characters in his famous novel *La Nausée* say that Santillana del Mar is "the most beautiful village in Spain."

Romantic literature was to play an important part in reassessing the artistic ensemble formed by Santillana del Mar. The evocative ruins, mediaeval streets, little squares and ancestral homes attracted the interest of Romantically-inspired poets. Later, writers such as Benito Pérez Galdós, Emilia Pardo Bazán, Miguel de Unamuno and José Ortega y Gasset —among others— wrote superb passages devoted to Santillana del Mar. In *El libro de Santillana (The Book of Santillana),* Lafuente Ferrari says that the author of *Episodios Nacionales* was the real discoverer, in literature, of this fine town in the province of Santander.

Through a character in one of his novels, Ricardo León made the following description of Santillana del Mar: "When he reached a slope in the path, Santillana appeared before his eyes, there at the foot of the valley, standing out amidst the clearings of the trees and ivy, with the colour of parchment, gold and amber that is acquired by stones

The Collegiate
Church: cloister.

A view of the
cloister.

Details of various capitals.

An original view of the cloister. ▷

hermit people? / What became of your Marquis, distinguished / in the Muses and in arms?'').

Another poet, José del Río Sáinz, says in his *Elegía de Santillana:*

> *Un nido viejo y agreste*
> *como éste,*
> *es lo que a Dios pido yo.*

(''An old, rural nest / such as this / is what I ask of God.'')

Other, contemporary, poets have dedicated poems to Santillana del Mar;

they include Ramón de Garcíasol, José Hierro and Gerardo Diego (who, with the Argentinian Borges, won the Cervantes Prize in 1979).

The town's origins apparently correspond to the foundation of one of the monasteries endowed in the mid-8th century, when the Spanish Christians organised their resistance against the Arabs. The settlement first took the name Concana, later Planes; finally, in the 11th century, it became known as Sancta Illana, which is derived from Sancta (Saint) Juliana, the Virgin and Martyr who died in Nicomedia,

A beautiful shot of the cloister.

Bithynia. Her remains were brought to the Iberian Peninsula in the 6th century and inhumed in a monastery in Santillana del Mar.

The town played an important rôle throughout the High Middle Ages. Its period of greatest splendour was initiated when Santa Juliana Monastery became a Collegiate Church, and embraces the 11th-12th centuries and the beginning of the 13th-14th; the decline began in the 15th century, which saw the struggles between the Mendoza and Manrique families (Don Iñigo López de Mendoza, the first Marquis of Santillana and author of *Serranillas,* belonged to the former).

THE COLLEGIATE CHURCH

This the most remarkable monument in Santillana del Mar, a town of monuments par excellence. The Collegiate Church was originally a monastery devoted to Santa Juliana. There is no documentary evidence of the date when the remains of this Virgin Martyr were actually transferred to Spain, but the popular tradition indicates that the event occurred in the 6th century. Popular devotion to Santa Juliana gave rise to the foundation of the monastery bearing her name; there are documents demonstrating its existence in the 10th century. No remains of this ancient monastery survive today: the Collegiate Church with the same dedication was built on its site in the 11th century.

The building we see today dates from the 12th century and constitutes an extraordinary specimen of Romanesque art. The church was built after the previous one, possibly Mozarabic, was demolished. The present-day church is made up of a nave and two nave-aisles; the interior is reached via an extensive courtyard, where the cemetery was formerly located. There are four monolithic columns supporting capitals topped by archivolts; and the porch displays a 17th-century pediment with, in the centre, a figure depicting S Juliana. A loggia, also 17th-century, forms the exterior wall of the right-hand nave-aisle. There is a remarkable Romanesque tower; and very beautiful pairs of windows in the transept. Backing onto the exterior of the church in this part are a house and a chapel (now the sacristy), both dating from the 18th century.

In the interior of the church the central nave is higher and longer than the nave-aisles; there are also three semicircular apses. Santa Juliana's tomb is in the centre of the church. The cupola stands above the transept; like the vaults of the nave, it has been altered. The very beautiful Romanesque capitals, dating from the early 12th century, display decorative stone carvings depicting soldiers fighting on horseback and on foot, spirals, small heads of animals, Biblical themes, botanical motifs, several men holding a cask, etc. As well as the capitals, the artistically-sculptured dados are also very interesting.

S Juliana's tomb, located in the centre of the nave, is protected by a 16th-century wrought-iron screen; the tombstone with a reclining figure of the saint is considered to be a popular 15th-century work. The effect of the position of Santillana del Mar's patron saint's tomb in the middle of the church is as impressive as it is evocative.

The Collegiate Church: reredos *of the high altar.*

Various views of the interior of the Collegiate Church and a fine perspective of the cloister.

Doña Fronilde's is another interesting tomb, situated in the transept. It is supported by figures of lions and features an artistically-carved slab attributed to the 12th century.

Valuable objects from different periods are conserved on the high altar of the Collegiate Church: special mention should be made of the Romanesque figures of four Apostles, carved in stone, which must have formed part of a group —with all the Apostles— that was apparently situated in the church's

A detail of the high altar: polychrome wooden figures of S Luke the Evangelist and his symbol, the bull.

Calle del Río, with the Collegiate Church in the background.

west doorway. These carvings date from the late 12th century and their author is anonymous: he may have been a French sculptor resident in Santillana for a while, for the style is very similar to that of other sculptures kept in Avila and Carrión de los Condes and held to be the work of a French master-craftsman.

Another very valuable piece is the reredos of the high altar, with figures depicting the Evangelists, scenes of the life of S Juliana before her martyrdom and others of the life of Christ: the Nativity, Epiphany, His entry into Jerusalem, and a Pietà.

There are various sculptures surrounding the reredos, probably dating from the 15th century; the paintings are early 16th-century.

The sacristy, near the tomb of Doña Fronilde, conserves numerous silver objects of great value; the most outstanding are a Gothic processional cross with fragments of the Lignum Crucis, a Romanesque reliquary, a fine candelabrum, three artistic chalices and two plates in the 16th-century Renaissance style.

We should also mention the large font in the baptistry chapel —decorated with a carving of Daniel surrounded by the lions—, several small baroque retables located between the nave and aisles, and a fine crucifix of the 18th-century Castilian school.

The cloister adjacent to the Collegiate Church is very interesting; there are several tombs of unidentified persons. The atmosphere is distinctly ghostly, of desolation and abandonment, symbolic of the transientness of human concerns. The enchanting precinct of the cloister seems to resound with the historical echo of voices from the past. It is easy to understand that this mysterious atmosphere of beyond the grave made a vivid impression on the Romantics' sensitivity. The visitor may feel as if surrounded by the spirits of Santillana's hidalgo inhabitanst, brought by magic back to life for a mo-

Plaza de Ramón Pelayo, an evocative square.

ment, struggling poetically — but in vain — to regain corporeity.... Contemplation of this silent, abandoned cloister may perhaps have inspired some of the Marquis of Santillana's beautiful poems, for example these verses:

Façade of the 'Casa de los Hombrones.

É podrás
Facer lo que non farás
Desamado

Or these verses:

Si dixieres por ventura

A charming view of the Plaza Mayor.

Main front of the beautiful 'Casa de los Tagle.'

Que la humana
Muerte non es cercana;
Gran locura
Es que piensse la criatura
Ser nascida
Para siempre en esta vida
De amargura.

Contemplating the abandoned tombs of unknown people who were perhaps powerful and esteemed in times past, one's spirit is assailed by melancholy; the visitor may well recall the sagacious philosophy contained in the Marquis of Santillana's compositions.

With regard to the cloister of the Collegiate Church, the artistic capitals on the left-hand side are outstanding. One of them depicts the Pantocrator, surrounded by evangelical emblems and figures of six of the Apostles. Another is decorated with figures of penitents, symbols of the sacrament of ordination, and scenes of the baptism and decapitation of S John. The next capital shows Daniel surrounded by the lions, his accusers being devoured by them, and the figure of a person lying on a bed. There is one with a fine carving of the Descent from the Cross. Even within the generally elevated quality of all this really extraordinary collection of capitals, one's attention is drawn to one with carvings of a lady, with a palm leaf in her hand, welcoming a gentleman.

'Infanta Paz' mansion, and 'Don Borja's Tower.'

The magnificent 'Gil Blas' Parador Nacional.

The capital depicting Samson fighting a lion is also very interesting. The figure of a lion struggling against a knight is the motif of another splendid example. Capital no. 11 features a dragon attacking a horse and angels fighting devils. The following capitals, from no. 12 to no. 19, depict fabulous beasts, botanical motifs, birds, etc. No. 20 shows S Michael weighing souls in a balance.

The capitals on the other sides of the cloister present plant motifs and appear to be of a later date than the left-hand side, which is considered to be late 12th-century.

The Romanesque reliefs adorning the corners of the cloister are of great in-terest. They depict the Pantocrator (re-taining traces of the original polychrome paint) holding a book in His left hand and making a gesture of bless-ing with the other; the Virgin Mary with the Child Jesus on her knees; and S Juliana vanquishing the devil. Not only the Pantocrator, but also the reliefs of the Virgin and Child and of S Juliana, are Romanesque carvings of great artistic merit.

The medallions, discovered when restoration work on the church vaults began in 1966, also deserve special mention. It seems that these artistic medallions made up part of the Romanesque cornice located in the southern part of Plaza de la Colegiata.

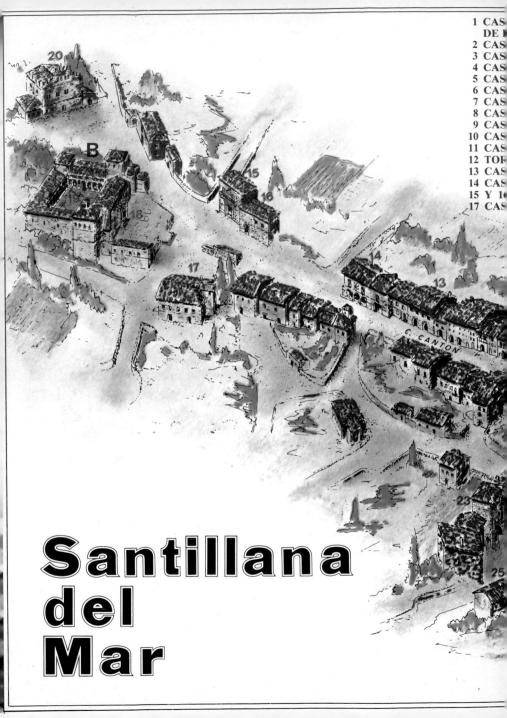

Santillana del Mar

'Don Borja's Tower' and 'El Merino Tower.'

A street lined with historic buildings. ▷

'DON BORJA'S TOWER'

The 'Torre de Don Borja' stands in Plaza de Ramón Pelayo, as does the 'Torre del Merino,' on the corner of Calle de las Lindas. 'Don Borja's Tower' is considered to be of mediaeval origins, although it forms part of a 15th-century building. This interesting tower/mansion has belonged to the Barreda family, to Doña Paz de Borbón, Princess of Bavaria, Isabella II's daughter, to Doña Mercedes de Baviera y Borbón, and to the Güell family.

This is one of the most characteristic monuments in Santillana del Mar.

'EL MERINO TOWER'

Popularly known as 'la Torrona,' this is considered to be the most representative monument in Santillana del Mar (after the Collegiate Church). The 'Torre del Merino' was built in the 14th century; spacious living-quarters were added in the 18th.

The ground-plan is square and the sturdy walls are of solid masonry, with ashlars at the corners. The three-storey edifice displays narrow loopholes and a beautiful pair of windows with round arches. It has now been converted into a Museum of Contemporary Art.

A typical street in Santillana.

THE MARQUIS OF BENEMEJIS' HOUSE

This is also the 'Casa de los Peredo-Barreda' and stands at the beginning of Calle de Santo Domingo. The majestic façade dates from the middle of the 17th century and displays an escutcheon with the Peredo family's coat of arms. The wrought-iron balconies are very fine.

The outstanding sections of the interior are the sumptuous drawing room and the library, considered to be one of the most important in the whole province. It was initiated by Don Blas María de Barreda y Horcasitas at the beginning of the 19th century and includes several in-cunabula, very interesting manuscripts and valuable genealogical collections.

THE HOUSE AND ARMS OF THE 'HOMBRONES'

The 'Casa de los Hombrones,' in Calle del Cantón, is one of the most popular houses in Santillana del Mar and belongs to the Villa family. It boasts a large baroque escutcheon popularly named after the 'Hombrones': two colossal warriors holding a coat of arms. In the middle, a plumed helmet crowns the Villa family's spread-eagle enclosed by the motto "Una buena muerte honra toda la vida" —"A good death gives honour to a whole life." This escut-

Plaza de las Arenas, and the apses of the Collegiate Church.

cheon serves to sum up the hidalgo character of Santillana del Mar, the pride of the town.

OTHER MONUMENTS

Within the general physiognomy of Santillana del Mar —characterised by the existence of an extraordinary number of monuments —special mention is due to the following: a late-15th-century house belonging to the Marquis of Benemejis, in Calle de Santo Domingo, retaining beautiful, very high, rectangular windows; the 'Casa (House) de los Villa,' situated opposite the previous building, where the 18th-century main front, with semicircular balconies,

features an artistic escutcheon with the arms of the Villa, Cos, Bracho and Bustamante families; and the 'Casa de Gómez Estrada,' at the beginning of Calle de la Carrera —this is a typical house of hidalgos of modest standing, displaying small windows and the family arms. Also 'Casa de la Cueva' and the 18th-century 'Casa de Bustamante,' both with fine coats of arms on their façades; the 15th-century 'Casa de los Velarde,' which has an ogive entrance arch and small rectangular windows; and the 'Casa de los Valdivieso' (now the Hotel Altamira), at the end of Calle del Cantón, with an 18th-century main front presided over by a beautiful escutcheon. We should also mention 'Casa

Calle de Santo Domingo.

de Leonor de la Vega,' at the junction of Calle del Cantón and Calle del Racial, considered to have been the Marquis of Santillana's mother's mansion— the beautiful, restrained façade is adorned by the Vega family's coat of arms; the 18th-century 'Casa de Cossío,' with a large escutcheon on the main front and a splendid wrought-iron balcony; and 'Casa de Quevedo,' to the left of the last-mentioned, which belonged to the famous writer and poet Don Francisco de Quevedo y Villegas. The 18th-century 'Archduchess Margaret of Austria's House' bears an escutcheon with the arms of the Barreda, Cossío, Velarde, Villa, Peredo and Ceballos families, and other renowned Santillana dynasties.

Other outstanding buildings within the town's ensemble of monuments include the Velardes' Mansion, a beautiful, extensively restored edifice conserving a certain Renaissance atmosphere, where the double windows and the Velarde family's coat of arms are particularly attractive; the 'Casa del Ayuntamiento' (Town Hall) with its balconies full of flowers; and the former prison, now the town's telephone exchange. Also 'Casa de los Estrada,' standing opposite the Parador de Turismo (luxury State hotel) in Calle de Juan Infante, with its old tower, now restored, an escutcheon with the family eagle, and a superb gallery; and several other ancestral homes lining Calle de Juan Infante.

The whole town offers to the visitor's eyes the façades of ancestral homes where the coats of arms attest to their venerable history.

'Regina Coeli' Monastery is also very interesting; the Diocesan Museum is now accommodated in it. The monastery was endowed by Don Alvaro de Velarde, in 1589, to house a community of Dominican monks; in 1825 nuns of the order of S Clare took their place. The church and the beautiful cloister, in the style of Juan de Herrera, have recently been restored. The Diocesan Museum's collections are installed in the two-storey cloister, with several statues and works of popular jewellery whose main interest lies in the ingenuousness of the sentiments that inspired them. On the ground floor there is an interesting exhibition of photographs relating to the Romanesque style in the province of Santander. The exhibits on the first floor include several painted panels, a collection of images from various churches —Suano, Barrio and Lebeña, among others— and the Count of Agüero's tomb.

The Dominican monastery, founded by Don Alonso Gómez del Corro in the 18th century, is similarly of undoubtable interest. Its church retains the coats of arms of the founder's family and those of the House of Mendoza Luna.

In Campo de Revolgo, on the road leading south towards Altamira cave, the visitor will encounter the 'Casa de los Tagle.' Its beautiful façade displays a monumental baroque escutcheon with the family arms: a knight impaling a dragon on his lance, in the presence of a praying figure. Inside the building the handsome hallway is outstanding,

as also several rooms with period furniture and meritorious paintings. This important mansion belongs to the heirs of the Marchioness de Las Forjas.

Façade of one of the town's beautiful houses.

'Casa de los Velarde.'

The monumental escutcheon of the house popularly known as 'Casa de los Hombrones.'

An angle of Plaza del Ayuntamiento ('Town Hall Square').

PARADOR NACIONAL DE GIL BLAS

The 'Gil Blas' Parador Nacional de Turismo (luxury State hotel) occupies an old building that belonged to the Barreda-Bracho family, situated at the entrance to Calle de Juan Infante and displaying a handsome coat of arms on the main front. The Parador bears the name of the protagonist of Lesage's famous novel entitled *Gil Blas de Santillane*. This popular character of picaresque literature says of himself: "Before reading the story of my life, listen to a tale I shall tell you, dear reader. Two students were travelling together on foot from Peñafiel to Salamanca: feeling tired and thirsty, they sat down next to a wayside spring. They saw a tombstone, carved with these words: 'Here is buried the soul of Pedro García, scholar.' One of the students burst out laughing, and exclaimed, 'What an amusing blunder! Here is buried the soul! How then, a soul can be buried? I'd like to be informed who was the most ignorant author of so ridiculous an epitaph!' When this student had gone, his fellow, who was rather more judicious and reflective, said to himself, 'There is a mystery here, and I must not leave this place until I have uncovered it.' He contrived to raise the slab and found a hundred ducats in a bag, with these words in Latin: 'I declare you my heir, whoever you may be, who have had the wit to understand the true meaning of the inscription; but I charge you to put this money to better use than I did.''

Thus commence the adventures of the character, created by Lesage, who gave his name to the Parador Nacional of Santillana del Mar. The construction of this powerfully evocative building was carried out over three different periods: their respective architectural styles can

Calle del Racial, with the countryside in the background.

The Marquis of Santillana's house.

A view of Calle del Cantón.

be discerned in the structure of the Barreda-Brachos' stately old mansion. The main front, of magnificent masonry, displays several large, artistic windows with grilles, and elegant balconies. The stone of the façade is protected by broad eaves.

After crossing the threshold, one reaches a very large hallway displaying a mosaic of stones, in the old *montañés* (Santander province) manner. In the interior of the Parador special mention is due to the sumptuous drawing room on the first floor, of majestic design. Valuable paintings, period engravings, old chests and other decorative items embellish the halls and bedrooms of the hotel, which is undoubtably one of the most charming, comfortable Paradores in Spain.

THE CHARM OF THE STREETS AND SQUARES

It is a real pleasure to stroll through the evocative streets and squares of the town. The visitor constantly encounters ancient mansions with noble façades bearing aristocratic coats of arms; one has the sensation of establishing a miraculous spiritual and visual contact

Close-up of Calle de Juan Infante.

with the historical countenance of the past.

The two authorities —royal and ecclesiastical— that governed the destiny of Santillana del Mar in the Middle Ages manifest their influence on the town's structure in its two main squares: Plaza de Ramón Pelayo and Plaza de la Colegiata. The 'Torre del Merino,' the military and administrative hub of Santillana, stands in the former; while in the latter, the Collegiate Church was originally the site of the monastery of Santa Juliana, and thus the religious centre.

Two main streets lead off from the Barreda crossroads: Calle de Juan Infante, which leads to the 'Torre del Merino,' on the left; and, on the right, the streets called Santo Domingo, Carrera, Cantón and del Río — really one street, running past the main front of the Collegiate Church.

These streets and the two squares mentioned earlier are the most interesting in Santillana del Mar, both for the monuments and ancestral homes situated in this part of the town and by virtue of the fact that this is its historical and artistic centre.

If one heads south from the Barreda crossroads, one reaches the area where the 'Regina Coeli' and the Dominicans' monasteries stand; and also Campo de Revolgo, with its grove of trees and the important 'Casa de los Tagle.' It may perhaps have been here, in the shade of the trees of Campo de Revolgo, that the Marquis of Santillana composed the beautiful poem that begins with these verses:

Por una gentila floresta
De lindas flores e rosas
Vide tres damas fermosas
Que de amores han reqüesta.
Yo con voluntad muy presta

A beautiful corner in Calle del Río.

Me llegué a conosçellas:
Començó la una dellas
Esta canción tan honesta:
    Aguardan a mi:
    Nunca tales guardas ví.
Por mirar su fermosura
Destas tres gentiles damas,
Yo cobríme con las ramas,
Metíme só la verdura.
La otra con grand tristura
Començó de sospirar
E deçir este cantar
Con muy honesta messura:
    La niña que amores há,
    Sola ¿cómo dormirá?...

Calle de las Lindas is one of the most attractive streets in Santillana: a narrow, typically mediaeval little thoroughfare onto which gives the façade of the 'Torre del Merino.' Here one may call to mind the fierce struggles between the factions of hidalgo families who disputed the enjoyment of power in the township. There could be no better scene for such flights of the imagination. One can feel carried away by conjuring up the history of the time when the Mendoza and Manrique dynasties competed for possession of the lands of Santillana. Out of the mist of centuries

A view of Calle del Río.

appears the historic figure of Doña
Leonor de la Vega, the mother of Don
Iñigo López de Mendoza, first Marquis
of Santillana and author of *Serranillas...*
Opposite the 'Torre del Merino,' in Calle
de las Lindas, is a suitable place to recall
the poet and Marquis, reciting his *Deçir
de Enyego López de Mendoça:*

> *Yo mirando una ribera,*
> *Vi venir por un grand llano*
> *Un ome que cortesano*
> *Paresçia en su manera:*
> *Vestía ropa extrangera,*
> *Fecha al modo de Bravante,*
> *Bordada, bien roçegante,*

Passante del estribera.
Traía al su diestro lado
Una muy fermosa dama,
De las que toca la fama
En superlativo grado:
Un capirote charpado
A manera bien estraña,
A fuer de alta alimaña
Donosamente ligado.

The poet ends with these verses:

> *Bien debo loar Amor,*
> *Pues todavía*
> *Quiso tornar mi tristor*
> *En alegría.*

("Well must I praise Love, / For it still /
Tried to turn my sadness / Into joy.")

ALTAMIRA CAVE

Located 2 km from Santillana del Mar,
this cave constitutes one of the most
important monuments of prehistoric art
in the world. It conserves, possibly in
the best condition of all those known,
cave paintings of exceptional artistic
quality, depicting —with extraordinary
charm and vivacity— figures of horses,
bison, deer, wild boars and other
animals, in red, ochre and black tones.
Don Miguel de Unamuno wrote the
following verses in a splendid poem
about Altamira cave:

Cavernario bisonteo,
tenebroso rito mágico,
introito del culto trágico
que culmina en el toreo.
¡Ay, cueva de la Altamira,
libre de sol, santo coso
del instinto religioso
que a un cielo de carne aspira!
España de antes de Adán
y de Eva y su paraíso,
cuando a los hombres Dios quiso
dar hambre por todo pan...

According to experts, the paintings on
the ceiling of the large natural room of
Altamira cave —considered to be "the
Sistine Chapel of quaternary art"—
were executed some 13,800 years
before Christ. Altamira cave was
discovered by chance in 1868, by
Modesto Cubillas Pérez, who lived in
Puente San Miguel and was a tenant

One of the painted bison at Altamira.

farmer for the landowner Don Marcelino S. de Sautuola. Seven years later, Sautuola began to prospect in the depths of the grotto, in search of traces of a settlement by prehistoric man. In 1879 his little daughter María Sáinz de Sautuola, who was accompanying him on one of his expeditions, discovered by chance the famous paintings on the ceiling of one of the chambers in Altamira cave. Sautuola published a booklet entitled *Brief Notes on Some Prehistoric Objects in the Province of Santander,* reproducing the paintings at Altamira for the first time. The discovery was received with mistrust and incredulity in the world of prehistorical research until, fourteen years after Sautuola's death, the French scholar E. Cartailhac (who had made discoveries similar to those at Altamira, in a cave in the Dordogne, France) confirmed that he had been right. Cartailhac's article, published in *L'Anthropologie,* a journal that he edited in Paris, was called *Les cavernes ornées de dessins. La grotte d'Altamira. Mea-culpa d'un sceptique.*

King Alfonso XIII visited Altamira cave in the year 1920; five years later the

The figure of a bison painted on the natural relief of the rock.

Altamira *Patronato* (Board of Trustees) was created, under the presidency of the Duke de Alba. In 1961 an underground room was inaugurated in the National Archaeological Museum in Madrid, with a photographic survey of Altamira, carried out by the *Deutsches Museum* of Munich.

The cave at Altamira comprises a vestibule and a gallery. In the painted chamber, the walls and ceiling are decorated with depictions of different animals —mainly bison, horses, a hind and a wild boar— taking advantage of the relief of the rock so as to model the figures. The paintings date from the Solutrean and early Magdalenian periods; the depictions of the animals are astonishing for the vigour and dynamism with which they were executed.

Altamira cave has been magnificently adapted for visits and electric light has been installed, making it possible to view the smallest details of the paintings in all comfort. By the side of the grotto there is a small museum conserving prehistoric finds from Altamira. The cave has been classified as a National Monument.

The interior of a cave at Puente Viesgo 35